Pebble®
Plus

Halloween Fun

Jack-o'-Lanterns

by Megan Cooley Peterson

Consulting editor: Gail Saunders-Smith, PhD

CAPSTONE PRESS
a capstone imprint

Pebble Plus is published by Capstone Press,
1710 Roe Crest Drive, North Mankato, Minnesota 56003
www.capstonepub.com

Library of Congress Cataloging-in-Publication Data
Peterson, Megan Cooley.
Jack-'o-lanterns / by Megan Cooley Peterson.
pages cm.—(Pebble Plus. Halloween Fun)
Includes bibliographical references and index.
Summary: "Simple text and full-color photographs describe jack-'o-lanterns"—Provided by publisher.
ISBN 978-1-4765-2180-0 (library binding)
ISBN 978-1-4765-3491-6 (eBook PDF)
1. Jack-o-lanterns—Juvenile literature. 2. Halloween—Juvenile literature. I. Title.
GT4965.P4 2013
394.2646—dc23   2013006882

Editorial Credits
Jeni Wittrock, editor; Heidi Thompson, designer; Wanda Winch, media researcher; Jennifer Walker, production specialist

Photo Credits
Images by Capstone Studio: Karon Dubke, except: Dreamstime: Vitaliy Rozhkov, Halloween icons;
Shutterstock: olga.lolipops, border; XNR Productions, 9

Note to Parents and Teachers

The Halloween Fun set supports social studies standards related to holidays and culture. This
book describes and illustrates jack-o'-lanterns. The images support early readers in understanding
the text. The repetition of words and phrases helps early readers learn new words. This book also
introduces early readers to subject-specific vocabulary words, which are defined in the Glossary
section. Early readers may need assistance to read some words and to use the Table of Contents,
Glossary, Read More, Internet Sites, and Index sections of the book.

Printed in the United States of America in North Mankato, Minnesota.
032013   007223CGF13

Table of Contents

Glowing Eyes

Eerie eyes glow in the dark.

Is it a monster? No!

It's a jack-o'-lantern!

Making jack-o'-lanterns is a fun

way to celebrate Halloween.

A jack-o'-lantern is a pumpkin
with a face. People carve
or paint faces on jack-o'-lanterns.
A candle burning inside a carved
pumpkin makes it glow.

The First Jack-o'-Lanterns

The Celts carved the first jack-o'-lanterns thousands of years ago. The Celts were people who lived in England, Ireland, Scotland, and France.

Say Celt: KELT

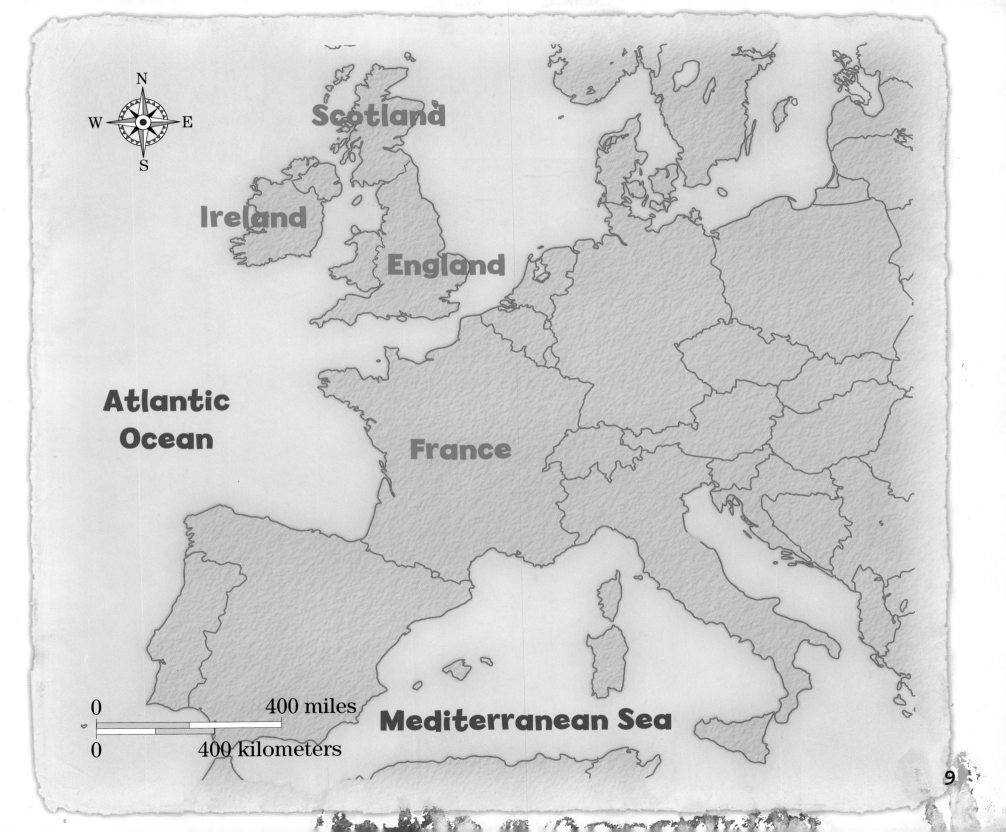

Scotland

Ireland

England

Atlantic
Ocean

France

Mediterranean Sea

400 miles

0

0

400 kilometers

The Celts believed spirits

returned to Earth on October 31.

They carved spooky faces

into turnips to scare away

bad spirits.

Stingy Jack

The name jack-o'-lantern comes from the Irish legend of Stingy Jack. His ghost roamed the earth. To light his way, Jack carried a turnip lantern.

To scare away Jack, the Irish carved turnips. Many Irish people moved to the United States in the 1800s. They used pumpkins, which were easier to carve.

Carving Jack-o'-Lanterns Today

Today we carve jack-o'-lanterns

at Halloween. Pumpkins can be

large or small, smooth or bumpy.

They come in many colors, like

red, white, and spooky green.

To carve your jack-o'-lantern,

first ask an adult for help.

Cut off the top of the pumpkin.

Then scoop out the pulp.

Draw a face on the outside of your pumpkin with a marker. Have an adult cut out the pieces. Drop in a candle, and wait for the screams!

Painted Jack-o'-Lantern

Looks like this jack-o'-lantern ate too much Halloween candy!
Grab a pumpkin, some paint, and get ready to have some spooky fun.

What You Need

newspaper

paintbrushes

lime green and black acrylic paints

candy corn

To Make

1 Set your pumpkin on some newspaper.

2 Paint the pumpkin green. Paint the stem black. Let dry.

3 Set your pumpkin on its side. You'll use the stem for its nose. Paint black eyes above the stem. Paint a large black oval for a mouth below the stem.

4 Spread candy corn out on the ground below the mouth.

Glossary

carve—to cut a particular design into a pumpkin

celebrate—to do something fun on a special day

eerie—strange and frightening

ghost—a spirit of a dead person believed to haunt people or places

legend—a story handed down from earlier times

pulp—the fleshy part of a fruit; pumpkin seeds are found in the pulp

roam—to wander

spirit—the soul or invisible part of a person; some people believe the spirit leaves the body after death

turnip—a white or yellow root vegetable with a round shape

Read More

Aloian, Molly. *Halloween*. Celebrations in My World. New York: Crabtree Pub. Company, 2009.

Johnson, J. Angelique. *Making a Jack-o'-Lantern, Step by Step*. Step-by-Step Stories. Mankato, Minn.: Capstone Press, 2012.

Schuette, Sarah L. *Halloween Hunt: A Spot-It Challenge*. Spot It. Mankato, Minn.: Capstone Press, 2011.

Internet Sites

FactHound offers a safe, fun way to find Internet sites related to this book. All of the sites on FactHound have been researched by our staff.

Here's all you do:

Visit *www.facthound.com*

Type in this code: 9781476521800

Super-cool stuff! Check out projects, games and lots more at www.capstonekids.com

Index

Word Count: 219
Grade: 1
Early-Intervention Level: 16